BLAZERS

WEAPONS OF WAR

WEAPONS OF THE
Middle Ages

by Matt Doeden

Reading Consultant:
Barbara J. Fox
Reading Specialist
North Carolina State University

Content Consultant:
John C. Hendrickson
Adjunct History Professor
Minnesota State University, Mankato

Capstone
press®

Mankato, Minnesota

Blazers is published by Capstone Press,
151 Good Counsel Drive, P.O. Box 669, Mankato, Minnesota 56002.
www.capstonepress.com

Library of Congress Cataloging-in-Publication Data
Doeden, Matt.
Weapons of the Middle Ages / by Matt Doeden.
p. cm. — (Blazers. Weapons of war)
Includes bibliographical references and index.
Summary: "Describes the weapons used in battles during the Middle Ages,
including siege weapons and weapons of hand-to-hand combat" — Provided
by publisher.
ISBN-13: 978-1-4296-1969-1 (hardcover)
ISBN-10: 1-4296-1969-4 (hardcover)
1. Weapons — History — Juvenile literature. 2. Siege warfare — Juvenile
literature. I. Title.
U800.D63 2009
623.4'41 — dc22   2007050935

Editorial Credits
Carrie A. Braulick, editor; Alison Thiele, designer; Jo Miller, photo researcher

Photo Credits
Alamy/Chris Howes/Wild Places Photography, 26; Alamy/Danita Delimont, 21
(battering ram); Alamy/North Wind Picture Archives, 6, 20; Art Resource, N.Y./Erich
Lessing, 11, 14 (crossbow); Art Resource, N.Y./HIP, 15 (spears), 29 (horse armor);
Art Resource, N.Y./The Metropolitan Museum of Art, 28 (chain mail); Art Resource,
N.Y./Victoria & Albert Museum, London, 14 (scimitar); Corbis/Bettmann 17; The
Granger Collection, New York, 5, 24, 25 (bottom left, top), 29 (kite shield, buckler
shield); The Image Works/The Board of Trustees of the Armouries/Heritage-Images,
8–9 (top); The Image Works/The Board of Trustees of the Armouries/HIP, 23, 28
(basinet helmet); The Image Works/The British Library/Topham-HIP, 27; The Image
Works/HIP/The Board of Trustees of the Armouries, 28 (English helm); The Image
Works/Topham, 7; James P. Rowan, 21 (ballista), 28 (plate armor); iStockphoto/
Henning Mertens, cover (sword and shield); Mary Evans Picture Library/Grosvenor
Prints, 10; Mary Evans Picture Library/Ins. of Civil Engineers, 13; Shutterstock/Aija
Avotina, cover (helmets and armor); Shutterstock/Andre Nantel, 15 (ball and chain);
Shutterstock/Anthro, 9, 15 (dagger); Shutterstock/Arturo Limon, 12, 15 (battle-ax);
Shutterstock/Bruce Amos, 29 (castle); Shutterstock/Dmitry Eliuseev, 21 (catapult);
Shutterstock/Dragan Trifunovic, 25 (bottom right), 29 (round shield); Shutterstock/
EchoArt, 8–9 (bottom); Shutterstock/Lagui, 18, 21 (trebuchet); Shutterstock/Marilyn
Volan, grunge background elements (all); Shutterstock/Nikita Rogul, 15 (mace);

Table of Contents

Bloody Battles

Crash! A huge rock smashes into a **castle**. Nearby, **knights** slash at enemies with swords. Wounded fighters fall to the ground everywhere.

castle — a large, heavily protected building where a ruler lived in the Middle Ages

knight — a European warrior of the Middle Ages who usually fought on horseback

War during the Middle Ages was bloody. This period of European history lasted from about AD 400 to 1400. There were no guns yet. But swords, axes, and bows were just as deadly.

WEAPON FACT

Knights used long spears called lances to knock enemies off their horses.

Blades, Battle-axes, and Bows

Almost every warrior carried a sword. Fighters slashed at enemies with wide broadswords. They jabbed at one another with narrow longswords.

WEAPON FACT

Many warriors carried small daggers as backup weapons.

9

longbow

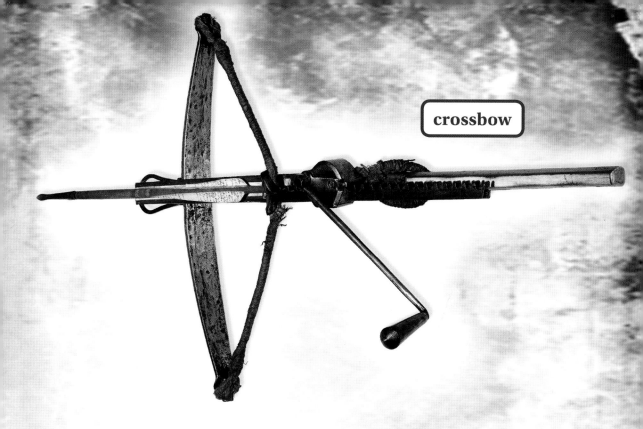

crossbow

Bows were threats even from long distances. The longbow had a **range** of more than 600 feet (180 meters). Crossbows couldn't shoot as far. But an arrow fired from a crossbow smashed through even the best **armor**.

range — the longest distance at which a weapon can still hit its target

armor — a protective covering worn by warriors during battle; in the Middle Ages, armor was usually made of leather or metal.

battle-ax

A warrior facing a battle-ax had to act quickly. Its sharp blade could cut off limbs. The war hammer was like a battle-ax. But it had a pick instead of a blade.

WEAPON FACT

Medieval is another word used to describe the Middle Ages.

war hammer

Handheld Weapons

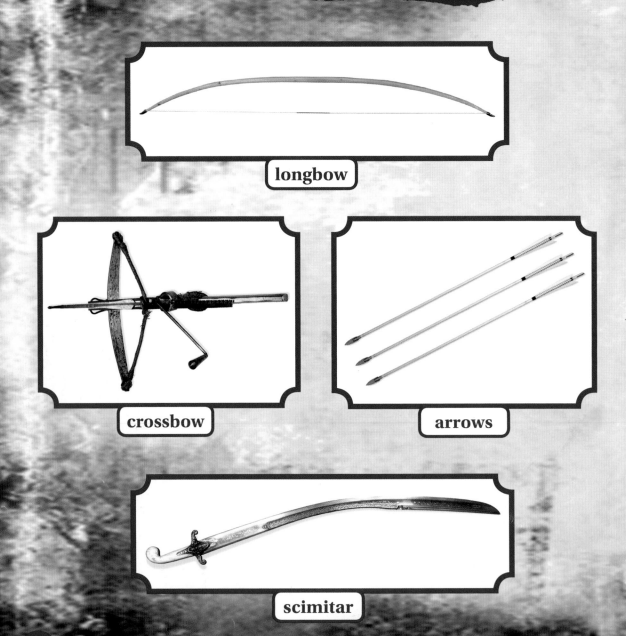

longbow

crossbow

arrows

scimitar

battle-ax

ball and chain

mace

spears

dagger

Siege!

Laying **siege** to a castle was
a huge job. Large throwing
machines called catapults sent
boulders sailing into castle walls.

siege — an attack on a castle, fort, or
other enclosed location

catapult

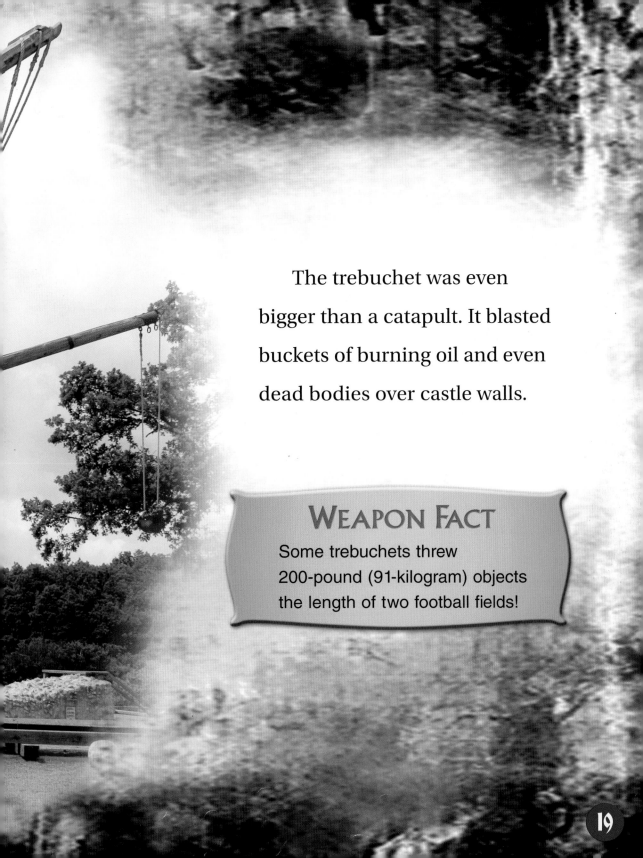

The trebuchet was even bigger than a catapult. It blasted buckets of burning oil and even dead bodies over castle walls.

WEAPON FACT

Some trebuchets threw 200-pound (91-kilogram) objects the length of two football fields!

WEAPON FACT

Siege towers often were
as tall as the castles.

Other weapons helped armies get inside castles. Battering rams knocked down doors. Ladders and siege towers helped attackers climb over walls.

Siege Weapons

**ballista
(giant crossbow)**

battering ram

catapult

trebuchet

21

Protection and Defense

Fighters needed all the protection they could get. **Chain mail** protected early knights. Later, knights wore plate armor made from solid metal sheets.

> **chain mail** — armor made from woven links of chain

WEAPON FACT

Knights often wore a cloth shirt called a surcoat over their armor. The surcoat showed their family symbol.

Warriors kept a tight grip on their shields. Triangle-shaped kite shields protected the upper body. Small, lightweight bucklers were easy to handle.

buckler shield

kite shield

round shield

WEAPON FACT

Bucklers were also called punching shields. They were used for attack as well as defense.

Castles had defenses too. **Moats** often surrounded them. Castles built on hills were hard to attack. Some castles of the Middle Ages still stand. They are reminders of an exciting yet dangerous time in history.

moat — a deep, water-filled trench built around the outside of a castle to prevent attacks

WEAPON FACT

Castle defenders sometimes threw
rocks or burning oil onto attackers.

Defenses

English helm

basinet helmet

chain mail

plate armor

horse armor

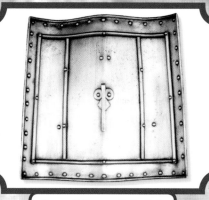

buckler shield

round shield

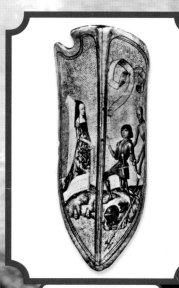

kite shield

castle moat

Glossary

armor (AR-muhr) — a protective covering worn by warriors during battle; in the Middle Ages, armor was usually made of leather or metal.

boulder (BOHL-dur) — a large rounded rock

castle (KASS-uhl) — a large, heavily protected building where a ruler lived in the Middle Ages

chain mail (CHAYN MAYL) — armor made from woven links of chain

knight (NITE) — a warrior of the Middle Ages who usually fought on horseback

limb (LIM) — a part of the body used in moving or grasping; arms and legs are limbs.

moat (MOHT) — a deep, water-filled trench built around the outside of a castle to prevent attacks

range (RAYNJ) — the longest distance at which a weapon can still hit its target

siege (SEEJ) — an attack on a castle, fort, or other enclosed location; a siege is usually meant to force the people inside the enclosed location to give up.

trebuchet (tre-byu-SHET) — a huge siege weapon that could toss heavy objects long distances; heavy counterweights provided a trebuchet's power.

Read More

Dargie, Richard. *Knights and Castles.* The Age of Castles. New York: PowerKids Press, 2008.

Eastwood, Kay. *The Life of a Knight.* Medieval World. New York: Crabtree, 2004.

Macdonald, Fiona. *Warfare in the Middle Ages.* Battle Zones. Columbus, Ohio: Peter Bedrick Books, 2004.

Internet Sites

FactHound offers a safe, fun way to find Internet sites related to this book. All of the sites on FactHound have been researched by our staff.

Here's how:
1. Visit *www.facthound.com*
2. Choose your grade level.
3. Type in this book ID **1429619694** for age-appropriate sites. You may also browse subjects by clicking on letters, or by clicking on pictures and words.
4. Click on the **Fetch It** button.

FactHound will fetch the best sites for you!

Index